WHO ARE YOU FOOLING?

DAVID LLOYD STRAUSS

BOOK FIVE OF THE GIGGLE YOGA SERIES

SECOND POCKET BOOK

Dedicated to everyone.

Especially the people I will never meet whose lives will be transformed by this tiny book.

Much Gratitude to Hawkwind Soaring

How BIG
is your bag
of excuses?

Who are you fooling?

Everyone knows, including you, that you are capable of so much more.

Do you really believe your own excuses or are you just playing it safe by hiding behind your self-inflicted fears and petty self-doubt?

What do you really want?

Do you want that new car?

New home?
New career?
New bike?
New boat?
New wardrobe?
New whatever…?

Or are you just hoping they will somehow fill a void for what is missing from your life.

Do you even know what you want?

Maybe it's not the new *whatever* that you want. Maybe you are looking for a feeling—a sense of connection.

To be loved.
Accepted.
Understood.
Appreciated.
Validated.

What if you could have both—the shiny new *whatever* and a sense of connection.

But if you don't know how to create that feeling from within, you will easily confuse accomplishment with connection.

Maybe the feeling you are looking for is the confidence to make things happen—to be in control of your life.

Perhaps it is the courage to be uncomfortable and different because that is what it will take to toss your bag of excuses and get serious about creating the life you truly desire.

Your excuses are not your truth. They are not who you are. They are pain avoidance.

But they can be your strength.

They are telling you that you are ready to make a change, to move in a new direction but you are afraid of taking the first step because of the messy uncertainty of doing something different.

Your excuses are showing you where you are weak, and where you need to learn and grow the most.

Maybe you are tired of fitting in and ready to step up and stand out.

Ready to discover your greatness and a whole new level of living.

Aren't you tired of your dreams being pictures of someone else living their dream?

Isn't it time for your dreams and goals to become your reality?

Perhaps you are ready, and you just need a nudge, or the permission to take that first step.

Maybe, just maybe, this book will give you the nudge you need to take the leap, the risk, to dive into the unknown part of yourself that is hungry for growth and advancement.

Perhaps your past has haunted you, stopped you from living and being the fullest and best version of yourself.

But wait. You are not your past.

You are not what you have done wrong.

You are not the sum of your mistakes and failures.

You are your choices.

You are what you choose to give your attention to.

You are what you choose to hold onto and what you release and forgive.

You cannot change what has happened. But you can change what it means to you.

Your past, present, and future are a mirror of your focus and attention—what you hold onto and what you let go of.

How you respond and what you learn from everything that happens to you is a choice—a decision.

Your decisions define you.

You are responsible for what you think, feel, and do—even if you don't do it consciously.

Other people may do things you dislike, but you choose your emotional response.

Look in the mirror right now and ask yourself one question.

Do you love you?

Do you like the person you have become?

If yes, then stop reading.

If no, then keep reading.

You are on this page because you answered no.

Keep reading.

What is it going to take for you to have the courage to stop judging yourself?

What is it going to take for you to embrace your uniqueness?

...to be unapologetically you?

...to accept 100% responsibility for the reality of your choosing?

Isn't it time to stop blaming, stop being a victim?

Isn't it time to start forgiving yourself—and others?

Isn't it time to start believing in yourself?

Isn't it time to start creating?

Isn't it time to start being the leader of your life?

Are you looking for love, happiness, joy, health, prosperity?

They are not far away.

They are not ahead of you, or a future destination.

They are a decision away.

They are you.

Here. Now.

In the moment.

By choice, if you choose.

Stop waiting, hoping, praying.

Start believing.

Start being.

Start doing.

Demonstrate your belief by doing something now.

Stamp out hesitation before it becomes fear.

Get in the driver's seat of your life.

Be the cause and the action.

Spark the change in your life.

By choice or neglect you have created the unfoldment of your life.

You are living in the reflection of your prior choices.

You can change the reflection. You can redefine you.

It will take courage and persistence, but you can do it.

You are fully capable of claiming complete, unhinged, unrestricted responsibility for your life.

It starts with a decision.

First stillness, then massive action and faith make it so.

Make a decision now.

Stop hesitating.

Stop postponing.

Stop wasting your potential.

What do you want to create?

Who do you want to become?

Make room for progress.

Let go of emotional anchors.

Toss habitual hesitations.

Disregard worn out excuses.

Let go of your old story.

Let go of situations that keep you trapped.

Let go of sticky, unhealthy relationships.

Let go of toxic emotional entanglements.

Let go of people who are not loyal to you.

Let go of self-limiting beliefs.

Let go of anything that is dragging you down.

Quit making excuses.

Quit buying your own excuses.

Let go and do not look back.

If you want to be happy, it is your responsibility.

If you want to be healthy, it is your responsibility.

If you want to be financially secure and abundant, it is your responsibility.

Whatever you want, it is your responsibility to shift your thinking and make it happen.

Be the voice and master of your destiny.

Decide to move forward in your chosen direction.

Don't worry about what other people think about you or your choices.

It is your life.

You have to live with yourself.

The only thing that matters is what you think and feel about yourself.

If you do not like the person you have become, then do something about it.

Make the decision to give yourself a fresh start.

It's your life.

Transformation is a choice.

Start now. Start where you are.

Start with what you have, what you know, and be willing to learn and grow.

If your spirit is broken from a painful past event, forgive and immerse yourself in a positive environment.

Raise your standards of what is and is not acceptable to you.

Renew your heart and soul.

Refresh your mind.

Only you can make that choice.

Once and for all, release yourself from the chains and shackles of your past.

Let go of your fears.

Let go of your anger, grudges, and resentments.

Accept responsibility by setting new standards for every area of your life.

Draw a line in the sand, walk away from your past, and step into your dreams—your truth.

Life is a blessing in disguise.

If something painful happens, look for the hidden lesson.

If you cannot find a lesson, create one.

Learn from it.

Move forward.

Forward is the only direction in life that is sustainable.

All else is an emotional trap.

If you are not moving forward, ask yourself one simple question.

What am I holding onto that is more important than the rest of my life—my happiness, my peace of mind?

Your entire life will transform when you have no choice but to move forward.

You cannot alter your past. But you can give yourself a fresh start by looking at your past with fresh eyes, with a fresh heart and mind.

When you are ready for growth and transformation, remember this.

You are not alone.

All the love and support are there for you, but it is up to you to ask and receive.

If hesitation is hindering your first step in a new direction, stop asking fear-based questions.

What if it doesn't work?

Instead, ask power questions.

What if it does work?

What if my life becomes my dream come true?

What if this moment is when it all comes together?

Be honest with yourself about your feelings, but do not make emotional pain your identity.

Feel the fear, doubt, sadness, loneliness, or emptiness, but do not live there. Make it your motivation for action.

Move on with your life.

You have to move on.

You must.

We all have to make sense of our past, reconcile our differences, and find that inner peace.

We all have to work through our choices, navigate our battles, and learn the lessons presented to us.

That is life.

Time heals all wounds, but you decide how long it takes.

Everyone chooses how long they hold onto something.

Forgive quickly.

The sooner you let go, the more life you get to live.

How about letting go right here, right now?

Why not?

What do you have to lose by liberating yourself from your grip on your past?

You are far more powerful than any challenge that life has presented to you.

You do not have to go at it alone.

Ask for help.

Seek counsel from people who have the awareness and results to guide you with wisdom.

Move forward.

Surround yourself with strong people who challenge you to learn and grow.

Surround yourself with people who encourage you, who believe in you.

Avoid the trap of indulging your emotions with people who drag you down, hold you back, or allow you to feel sorry for yourself.

Move forward by first looking forward.

To look forward, building confidence must be your priority.

You must learn to believe in yourself, your potential, your power to create.

You must learn to take action.

You must see yourself as having the same qualities as those who have what you desire.

Do everything you can to learn and grow and to become a confident, resilient person.

See yourself as worthy and deserving of your highest good.

Love yourself, forgive yourself, accept yourself for what you are now, and believe in what you can become.

Surround yourself with inspiring people who uplift your confidence and spirit.

Seek relationships that elevate your awareness and bring joy to your life.

Associate with people who expand your vision and enthusiasm.

Identify your tribe—the people and community that match your highest good.

If you cannot find your tribe, create one that resonates with your vision for yourself and your life.

Do not stand in judgment of what anyone has said or done to you or what you have done to yourself.

Be the first to forgive.

Take ownership of your life.

Reclaim your power over your thoughts and beliefs.

Surrender all blame.

Find reasons to be grateful.

You are not your past.

You are not a victim of anyone or anything unless you choose to be.

Stop looking outside yourself for answers that are only found within.

Stop playing hide-and-go-seek with love and happiness.

The courage, acceptance, and love you need to move forward is in your heart, waiting to be discovered and received.

You are the hero you are looking for.

Look at your life right here and right now—in this moment.

Do you stubbornly blame people and circumstances for your problems?

Are you fixated on the image in the rearview mirror of your life?

Do you have one foot in the past and the other facing forward, or do you have both feet forward, facing life head-on?

Are you forging ahead with confidence and a sense of certainty and purpose?

If not, why not?

Are you willing to release your grip on the past for the gift of peace of mind?

To move forward you must let go and look ahead.

Release mental or emotional blocks.

Surrender anger, resentment, guilt, shame.

Re-purpose your pain into a belief that empowers you.

Commit to personal growth.

There is no perfect moment.

There is no perfect decision.

You must create the circumstances if they do not yet exist.

You must create you.

No one else can do it for you.

Believe in yourself.

Believe in your potential

Believe in possibilities.

No one else can believe for you.

Learn from your shortcomings.

Victory is first disguised as failure.

Within every setback is a seed for greatness.

Your thoughts and beliefs, choices and actions, are the seeds.

That bag of excuses…

It is who you were, not who you are.

You are the master of your destiny.

You are whatever you choose to be.

Life is a mirror.

You are the image and the reflection.

You are the cause and the effect.

You are the on and the off.

You attract what you are.

Your thoughts are things.

You are the vibration of you…

…of life
…of happiness
…of love
…of whatever you choose to be or become
…of the great spirit of the universe.

Stop waiting.

Start doing.

There is no more time.

Each moment slips away faster than the last.

Before you know it, your lifetime will expire, and you will have no more tomorrows.

Dance my friend.

It is time to dance.

It is time to celebrate life, to return to the moment, to the eternal now.

It is time to be everything you are capable of being.

You are always nowhere.

"NowHere"

You are what you are looking for, but do not seek outwardly for you will not find.

Instead, breathe.

Reflect inwardly.

Rediscover your essence.

Give thanks.

Be the blessing.

There is only one you—one us.

Separate, but no separation.

We are.
I am.

The light.
The Love.
The mystery.
The magic.
The self.

All energetically connected.

Who are you fooling?

Yourself?

The fool is akin to the wise.

Up is down.

Sideways is straight ahead.

Giggle out loud.

Giggle often.

Do all this and more,
and you will become
the master of your life.

***

This, my friend,
is the path of
Giggle Yoga.

***

Pray. Give Thanks.
Giggle Out Loud.
Giggle Often.

GiggleYoga.com

About the Author

David Strauss became inspired to write after recovering from a rockfall to his head while visiting ancient Anasazi ruins in Chaco Canyon, New Mexico.

The turbulence of life is familiar to David. As a result of the in-fighting in his family after the death of his mother at a young age, David ran away from home when he was fifteen so that he could find peace, discover who he is, and build a life for himself.

To make sense of his life, David became an avid reader and world traveler. He discovered that life is a mirror. There is no truth outside of your own heart and mind.

You can travel all the continents, dive the deepest of oceans and ascend the highest peaks, and you will never find truth. The last place you look is where you will discover all that you are looking for—in your heart.

It is within your heart you will find gratitude, joy, healing, forgiveness, peace of mind, grace, abundance, and most importantly, your unique relationship with the divine.

Through the openness of his heart, David has become a globally known author, thought leader, and life strategist.

David has been seen on ABC, NBC, CBS, and FOX affiliate networks, Success Today, and presented at a private event at the United Nations Headquarters in New York City.

David believes that you are never truly free until you release all blame and accept complete responsibility for your entire life.

Follow David on social media.

@davidlloydstrauss
#davidlloydstrauss

COACHING: David's coaching programs can be found on his website.

SPEAKING Invite David to speak at your event. davidstrauss.com

David's other Books
  Dancing with Vampires
  Footsteps After the Fall
  Second Mouse Gets the Cheese
  What if Today Were the Day?

GET PUBLISHED. If you have a book in your heart and mind, David can help make it a reality.

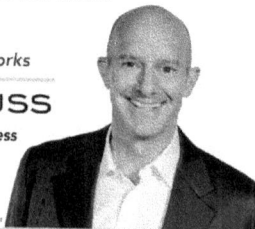

www.ingramcontent.com/pod-product-compliance
Lightning Source LLC
Chambersburg PA
CBHW071455070426
42452CB00040B/1534